The
FROG
Alphabet Book

. . . and other awesome amphibians

Jerry Pallotta • Illustrated by Ralph Masiello

Charlesbridge

This book is dedicated to Nina and Papa Owens.
—J. P.
Illustrations are dedicated to Dawn and the new baby.
—R. M.

Published by Charlesbridge
85 Main Street
Watertown, MA 02472
(617) 926-0329
www.charlesbridge.com

Library of Congress Cataloging-in-Publication Data
Pallotta, Jerry
    The frog alphabet book / by Jerry Pallotta; illustrated by Ralph Masiello
        p. cm.
    Summary: Introduces the letters of the alphabet by describing a frog or other amphibian
for each letter, from the Amazon horned frog to the zig-zag salamander.
    ISBN-13: 978-0-88106-463-6 (reinforced for library use)
    ISBN-10: 0-88106-463-7 (reinforced for library use)
    ISBN-13: 978-0-88106-462-9 (softcover)
    ISBN-10: 0-88106-462-9 (softcover)
1. Frogs—Juvenile literature. 2. Amphibians—Juvenile literature. 3. English language—
alphabet—Juvenile literature. [1. Frogs. 2. Amphibians 3. Alphabet.] I. Masiello, Ralph, ill.
II. Title.
QL668.E2P25 1991
597.6—dc20   90-80288

Printed in Korea
(hc) 10 9 8 7 6 5 4 3 2
(sc) 10 9 8 7 6 5 4 3

A a

A is for Amazon Horned Frog. This frog looks like it has sharp horns above its eyes, but the points are fake stems that help make the frog look like a leaf on the ground.

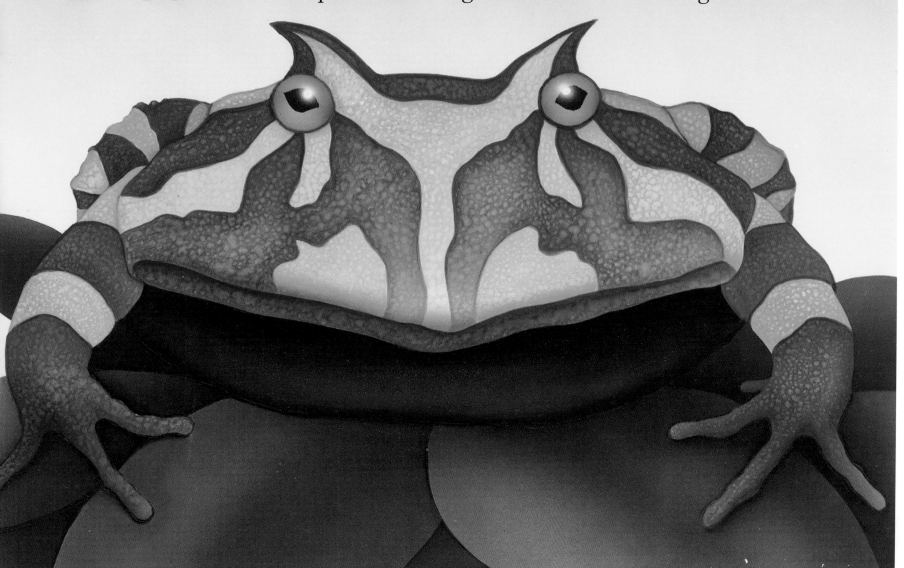

B b

B is for Blue-legged Strawberry Frog. This little frog may look cute but it is very poisonous. It looks like it is wearing blue gloves and blue stockings.

Be on the lookout for more poisonous frogs in this book.

Cc

C is for Crested Newt. All newts are salamanders, but not all salamanders are newts. The Crested Newt has a wavy crest along its back that makes it look different from other newts. Let's find another creature that begins with the letter C.

Cc

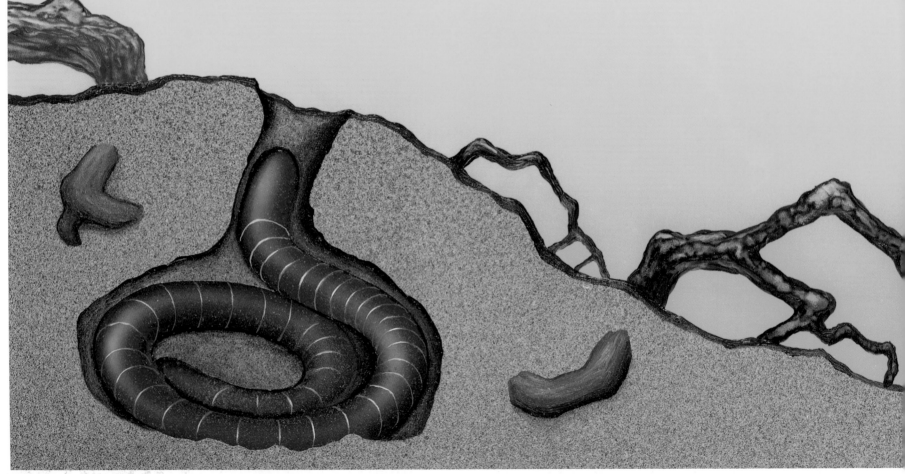

C is for Caecilian. Not too many people know about Caecilians. They are amphibians that have no arms and no legs. They look like snakes or worms.

D is for Dumpy Green Tree Frog. Some frogs live in water. Tree frogs climb and live in trees. If the Dumpy Green Tree Frog had friends, what do you think they would call him? "Hey, Dumpy."

This frog is from Australia.

D d

E e

E is for Eft. In the olden days newts were called Efts. Some newts are still called Efts when they leave the water to go live on land for a few years. The one on this page is a Red Eft.

F f

F is for Fire-bellied Toad. When this toad wants to scare off another animal, it leans its head back and shows its bright red belly. It may look like it has red nail polish on, but frogs do not have fingernails.

G g

G is for Goliath Frog. This is the biggest frog in the world, and it can jump farther than any other frog. It comes from Cameroon, Africa. The smallest frog in the world is the size of your baby fingernail.

H is for Hellbender. Hellbenders are giant salamanders that stay in the water. When fishermen accidentally catch Hellbenders, they sometimes cut their hooks and lines rather than touch them. Hellbenders are from the United States. They are also called Devil Dogs.

H h

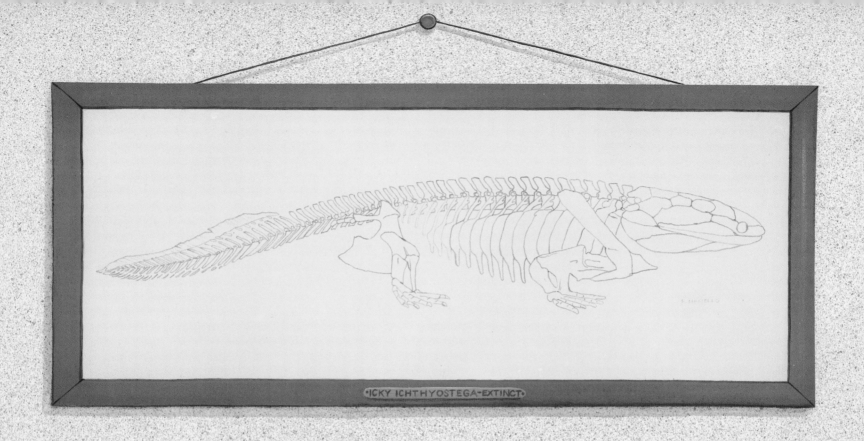

·ICKY ICHTHYOSTEGA-EXTINCT·

I i

I is for Ichthyostega. Millions of years ago the
Ichthyostega was the first creature to leave the water.
It was the first amphibian, but it is now extinct.

J is for Japanese Giant Salamander. This is the largest amphibian on earth. It is found at high altitudes in cold, shallow, swift-moving streams. The Japanese Giant Salamander is similar to a Hellbender but even bigger.

Jj

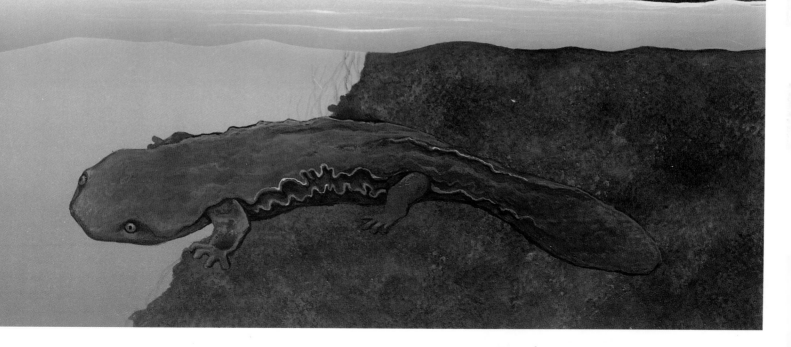

K k

K is the first letter of Knocking Sand Frog. The sand frogs of South Africa grow to be about an inch long. The Knocking Sand Frog makes a sound similar to someone knocking on a wooden door. Knock, knock. Who's there?

Ll

L is for Leopard Frog. The Leopard Frog has spots. It got its name from the spotted leopard. There are other North American frogs with mammal names—the Sheep Frog, Squirrel Tree Frog, Bull Frog, Mink Frog, and believe it or not, the Pig Frog.

M m

M is for Midwife Toad. When the mother Midwife Toad lays a string of eggs, the father Midwife Toad wraps the eggs around his hind legs and carries them on his back. This is an unusual way for a toad to protect its eggs. The Midwife Toad is from Europe.

N n

N is for Narrow-mouthed Frog. This frog does not hop or jump. It waddles. Its little mouth is perfect for eating ants and other small insects. The Narrow-mouthed Frog on this page can dig a hole with its back legs and bury itself.

O o

O is for Olm. The Olm has teeny-weeny legs. Its eyes are covered with skin, and it can barely see. Olms live in caves where there is hardly any light.

P p

P is for Poison-arrow Frog. Yikes! Poison-arrow Frogs! These are the most colorful of all amphibians. The bright colors are a warning for other animals to stay away. Hurry up, turn the page.

Q is for Quito Tree Frog. The Quito Tree Frog is green and therefore can hide from its enemies by blending in with the green leaves. This frog is from Ecuador.

Q q

R is for Red-eyed Tree Frog. This frog might be the most awesome of all the Central and South American rain forest frogs. If people keep cutting down the rain forests, these beautiful frogs will have no place to live.

R r

S s

S is for Spring Peeper. This is a noisy frog. Peep, peep. When lots of them are peeping nearby, peep, peep, it is hard to go to sleep. Peep, peep. This is one of the most common frogs in the United States. Peep, peep.

Let's read about other amphibians that begin with the letter S. Peep, peep, croak, peep, ribbit, peep, peep.

S is also for Surinam Toad. This amphibian is really different. Maybe it should be called the Pancake Toad. It looks as though a truck ran over it and flattened it.

S s

S s

S is also for Slimy Salamander. This salamander has no lungs. It breathes through its thin skin. When you pick it up, it leaves a sticky slimy goo on your hand that is really hard to wash off. Slimy salamander is its real name.

T is for Tadpole. Frogs lead a double life. When they hatch from their eggs, they become tadpoles. Tadpoles swim, and they breathe through their gills much like fish. Tadpoles eventually grow legs, lose their tails, and become frogs. Frogs breathe air through their lungs just like you do.

T t

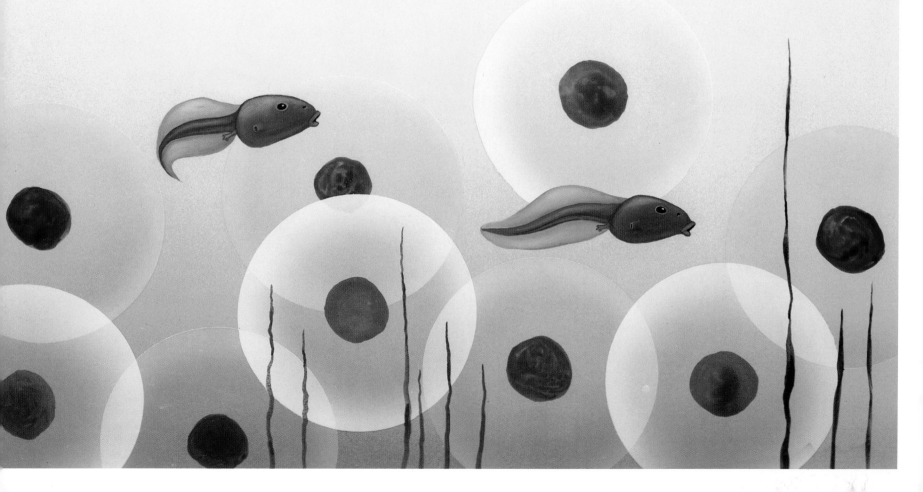

U u

U is for Undiscovered Frog. U is also for Unnamed Frog. All over the world there are dozens of frogs that have not yet been discovered. Maybe someday someone will find a new frog and call it the "Unbelievable Frog."

V v

V is for Valley and Ridge Salamander.
This salamander has a long tail and a
long name. It sounds as though people
could not decide whether to call
it a Valley Salamander or a
Ridge Salamander.

W is for Waterdog. Waterdogs and Mudpuppies are big salamanders. Their gills are on the outside of their bodies. Waterdogs do not bark and Mudpuppies seldom live in the mud, so it is hard to figure out how they got their names.

X **x**

X is for *Xenopus laevis*. *Xenopus laevis* is the
scientific name for Clawed Frog.
Clawed Frogs are excellent swimmers.
They have tiny claws on the ends of their
fingers that help them dig in the mud
for food.

Y is for Yosemite Toad. There is a National Park called Yosemite, and there is a toad called the Yosemite Toad. This toad can be found in the park. Toads are frogs that have adapted to living on land.

Y y

Z z

Z is for Zig-zag Salamander. We looked in a zillion places for a frog, toad, salamander, or newt that began with the letter Z. The Zig-zag Salamander has a zig-zag design along its back.

Now that we have finished the alphabet, maybe you would like to know that there are three living orders of amphibians:

1. *Anura* (those without tails): Frogs and Toads
2. *Caudata* (those with tails): Salamanders and Newts
3. *Apoda* (those without feet): Caecilians

There are no ocean amphibians.

THE END

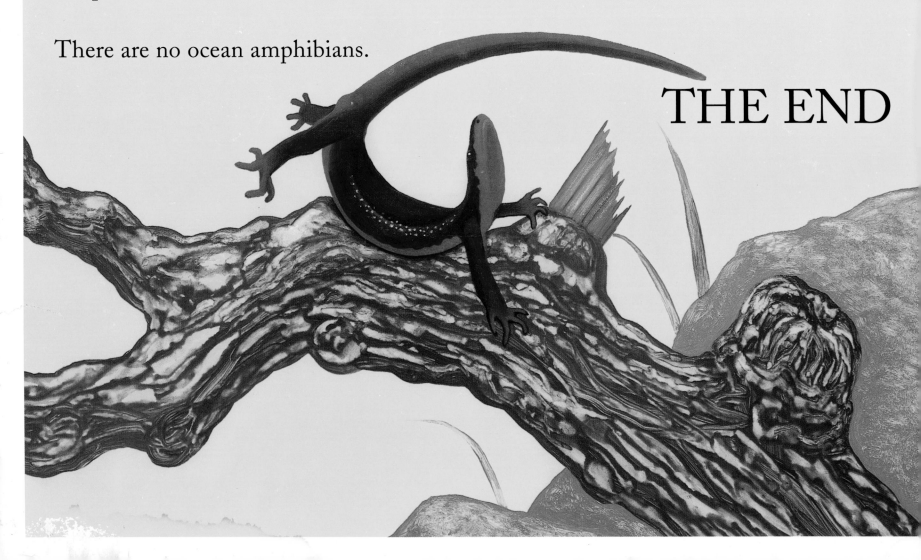